Resisting
Sin

7

The Single Sermon Series

Resisting Sin

Colin Hughes

Publishing
Angel
Climbing

Resisting Sin
Written by Colin Hughes

Edited by Lisa Soland
Text copyright © 2024 Colin Hughes

Most Scripture quotations are from the ESV® Bible (The Holy Bible, English Standard Version®), copyright © 2001 by Crossway, a publishing ministry of Good News Publishers. Used by permission. All rights reserved.

Published in 2024 by:
Climbing Angel Publishing
PO Box 32381
Knoxville, Tennessee 37930
http://www.ClimbingAngel.com

First Edition: July 2024
Printed in the United States of America

Front Cover Image: Joseph and Potiphar's Wife, c.1631 - Guido Reni
Graphic Design: Climbing Angel Publishing

ISBN: 978-1-956218-38-1
Library of Congress Control Number: 2024911903

This book is dedicated to West Park Baptist Church, who has taken me in as one of their own and has shown the love of God to me in ways I can never repay.

Resisting Sin

When studying the story of Joseph being tempted by Potiphar's wife in Genesis 39, we may think that we are able to resist temptations with our abilities and strategies alone. I am not referring to the more minor temptations in life, such as whether or not to resist eating an Oreo (or five) before dinner, whether to watch one more episode of your favorite show before you go to bed, or the temptation of sleeping in an extra hour instead of coming to church on Sunday morning. I'm talking about the temptations that can lead us to sin against God and walk away from His ways.

As we read these verses in Genesis 39, we will see that while battle plans and strategies are essential in resisting temptations, the true foundation for resisting temptations is our love for God and our desire to please Him. To overcome temptation, Christians must be rooted in a deep love for God above all else. So, as we read through this passage, let us not only think through the practical ways we can safeguard ourselves from sin; let us ultimately grow in our love for God.

Now Joseph had been brought down to Egypt, and Potiphar, an officer of Pharaoh, the captain of the guard, an Egyptian, had bought him from the Ishmaelites who had brought him down there. 2 The Lord was with Joseph, and he became a successful man, and he was in the house of his Egyptian master.3 His master saw that the Lord was with him and that the Lord caused all that he did to succeed in his hands.4 So Joseph found favor in his sight and attended him, and he made him overseer of his house and put him in charge of all that he had. 5 From the time that he made him overseer in his house and over all that he had, the Lord blessed the Egyptian's house for Joseph's sake; the blessing of the Lord was on all that he had, in house and field. 6 So he left all that he had in Joseph's charge, and because of him he had no concern about anything but the food he ate.

Now Joseph was handsome in form and appearance.7 And after a time his master's wife cast her eyes on Joseph and said, "Lie with me." 8 But he refused and said to his master's wife, "Behold, because of me my master has no concern about anything in the house, and he has put everything that he has in my charge.9 He is not greater in this house than I am, nor has he kept back anything from me except you, because you are his wife. How then can I do this great wickedness and sin against God?" 10 And as she spoke to Joseph day after day, he would not listen to her, to lie beside her or to be with her.

¹¹ But one day, when he went into the house to do his work and none of the men of the house was there in the house, ¹² she caught him by his garment, saying, "Lie with me." But he left his garment in her hand and fled and got out of the house.
(Genesis 39:1-12)

GOD'S PRESENCE IN JOSEPH'S LIFE

The first thing we notice in this text is that God's presence is in Joseph's life. In Genesis 37, Joseph was sold into slavery by his brothers to a group of people known as the Ishmaelites. So now, in Genesis 39, we see that Joseph has been brought down to Egypt, and a man named Potiphar, a high-ranking officer of Pharaoh, bought Joseph from the Ishmaelites and brought him to his house as a slave.

As we read verses 2-6, we see that, even in this dark and difficult situation, it is evident that God's presence is with Joseph. God blessed Joseph's hard work and caused everything Joseph did to succeed. God's presence in Joseph's life is so evident that even Potiphar, an Egyptian who was not a follower of YHWH (Yahweh), witnessed God's presence with Joseph. And because Joseph found favor with Potiphar, Potiphar made

Joseph the overseer of his house and everything he possessed.

Joseph's promotion was because of what God had been doing in Joseph's life and work. Yes, Joseph worked hard, but it was God who ultimately blessed his hard work. What a great story! If we stopped at verse 6, we would see that Joseph lived happily after. It all worked out for him. Praise God! This screenplay has such a great ending! Let's go ahead and roll the credits now, shall we?

But, if you are a Marvel movie fan like myself, you know that you must wait until the credits are over for the post-credit scene. When you read verse 7, you realize this story is not over and is not so "happily ever after" after all. We see Potiphar's wife, noticing Joseph's handsome appearance, set her eyes on him and ask him to sleep with her.

THE PURSUIT OF TEMPTATION

Joseph did nothing to provoke Potiphar's wife. Joseph didn't pursue her and go after his temptations like his brother Judah did in Genesis 38. Joseph didn't make a pass on Potiphar's wife or tempt her by posting a picture of himself on Instagram following a hard workout. He was just a good-looking guy minding his own business. Instead of looking for temptation and pursuing it, temptation pursued and went after him through Potiphar's wife, who had no regard for her marriage or God's way of living an obedient life. As sinful people, we may sometimes pursue our temptations, but because we live in a fallen world, the truth is that sometimes temptations also pursue us.

However, though Potiphar's wife relentlessly pursues him, Joseph does not give in. He does not accept this pursuit. Instead, he courageously refuses her offer and then provides the reasons as to why he is resisting.

THE REASONS FOR RESISTING SIN

In verses 8-9, we learn that Joseph is not just a good-looking guy; he's also quite an intelligent guy. Look at the reasons he gives as to why he refuses Potiphar's wife:

1. My master trusts me with his house and possessions.

2. My master has given me everything I could possibly need.

"I have a really good boss who trusts me and takes really good care of me." These are very good reasons for Joseph to be faithful to his boss.

If we think about it, when temptations come our way, there are many solid, practical reasons for refusing them as well—not just for the sake of our jobs but also for our friendships, families, spouses, and kids.

However, we also observe in this text that while Joseph provides practical reasons for refusing to sleep with Potiphar's wife, these are not his primary foundation for refusing. His foundation is seen at the end of verse 9.

THE LOVE FOR GOD THAT RESISTS SIN

As Joseph lays out his first two reasons for refusal, he then presents the ultimate, most important reason for rejecting Potiphar's wife.

"How then can I do this great wickedness and sin against God?"
(Genesis 39:9)

Joseph understands deeply that sleeping with Potiphar's wife would not only be a sin against his earthly master, but even more profoundly, it would be a sin against his Heavenly Master.

God has shown His presence and love for Joseph in his life, and as a response, Joseph recognizes that love and responds to God in love and obedience. In response to God's love, Joseph devotes himself to God. And because

Joseph loves God, he hates what God says is wickedness and evil. Joseph refuses to sleep with Potiphar's wife, not just because he doesn't want to get fired and put to death, but because he loves God. This love for God has taken root in his soul, and it is this love for God that drives his decisions.

But unfortunately, Potiphar's wife does not stop pursuing Joseph.

THE PERSISTENCE OF TEMPTATION

Even after Joseph refuses her offer, verse 10 says that Potiphar's wife spoke to Joseph "day after day," offering him to lie beside her and to be with her. Potiphar's wife, unyielding in her pursuit of Joseph, becomes more cunning in her advances. She no longer asks Joseph to sleep with her. Now, she invites him to lie beside her, to spend time with her.

This is what makes temptation so dangerous. It not only pursues; it persists. In obvious ways, yes, but also subtle ways. It can be as obvious as the offer: "Lie with me," or as subtle as "Hey, how are you? Come sit down, and let's talk about your day." And as we see in verse 12, temptation can try to trap you, grabbing you and cornering you as if you have no choice but to accept it. Sin and temptation will stop at nothing for you to give in to them. You might say "no" to the first temptation offer, but the temptation will return to you tomorrow. And the next day. "Day after day," the Bible says. And it will keep pursuing you, and you will have to keep resisting. You must fight both the obvious and the subtle offers of temptations.

THE WISDOM OF BOUNDARIES

Joseph not only declines Potiphar's wife's obvious offers but also establishes strategies and boundaries to prevent him from giving in to her subtle offers. He makes the right *big* decisions that help him resist and the right *small* decisions.

If we think of this in our own lives, it's not just the big decisions that lead us to sin and give in to temptation; it's also the more minor decisions that, over a long period, lead us to be weaker and more susceptible to sin. It's the subtle decision of looking at someone attractive for a few seconds longer than you should. Or continue watching that movie or show through a scene you know you should not be watching. Or clicking "like" on that picture of someone you have been following on social media. Or the subtle decision of driving the longer way home to pass the liquor store or bar you used to frequently visit. Or the decision to talk to yourself in the car about that situation or that person that makes you anxious or angry. These small decisions add up and make you gradually more susceptible to giving in to your temptations. One of my favorite Christian rappers, KB, put it like this in one of his songs entitled "Art of Drifting:"

"Every great fall's from 100 bad decisions."

We don't just succumb to a significant temptation after making one bad decision. It is the result of multiple small choices that lead us to give in to that significant temptation in our lives.

Joseph stuck to his devotion to God by being strategic. *"If she enters the room where I am, I'm moving to another room. I'm not even going to look at her. If she talks to me, I won't listen. I'm not going to lie beside her. I'm not going to sit beside her. I'm not even going to answer her questions."*

He kept resisting. He made the right *small* decisions that, as we see at the end of this passage, set him up to make the right *big* decision when it mattered most. In verse 12, the two of them are entirely alone. Potiphar's wife catches him by the garment, traps him, and begs him to sleep with her. But Joseph had resisted this far, so he ran and left his garment in her hand. He did not just subtly walk off. He runs! Joseph resists temptation through reason, foundational love for God, and intentional boundaries.

POINTS OF APPLICATION

We must not hope in our reason or in our boundaries in order to resist temptation.

When resisting temptation, it would be unwise for us to place all our trust into our reasoning and strategies. The Bible's teachings on humanity's nature are clear: since the sin of Adam and Eve, humanity has been cursed with a corrupt, sinful nature. This nature, driven by its own sinful desires, naturally drifts from God. We are naturally incapable of honoring God because we are naturally incapable of loving God.

Ephesians 2:1-3 talks about this natural state of humanity:

*And you were dead in the trespasses and sins in which you once walked, following the course of this world, following the prince of the power of the air, the spirit that is now at work in the sons of disobedience—among whom we all once lived in the passions of our flesh, carrying out the desires of the body and the mind, **and were by nature children of wrath, like the rest of mankind.***

God's Word does not just teach that we sin; God's Word teaches that we are sinners. We not only commit sins against God's Law and do things that are offensive to Him, but we do not love Him nor seek to honor Him. We might try to resist temptations with our reasons and strategies, but the problem is that our hearts desire those temptations more than they desire God, no matter the strategies we put in place.

I have a dog named Cooper. He's a fluffy, 80-pound Golden Doodle, and he is the best dog ever. I have often told people that I will never get another dog after Cooper because he is that great!

But Cooper has a fatal flaw—he likes digging holes beneath the backyard fence. And so there would be afternoons and evenings when I would let him out in the backyard to do his business, play with my stepdad's dog, and release some energy. But there would be afternoons or evenings when I would call Cooper to come inside from the backyard, but he wouldn't....because he was no longer in our backyard. He was in another backyard or on the other side of the fence leading to another neighborhood.

We had this problem with Cooper for close to two years. We had no idea why he would do it, and we had no idea how to fix it. We put down barriers and cinderblocks and gave him a shock collar. Yet through all that, Cooper would see this as a challenge and think, *"Hmm, okay. I can work with this."* Then he would dig another hole and take off like a thief in the night! Thankfully, he doesn't do this anymore, but I'm sure you can imagine how stressful this was!

Whatever temptation was drawing Cooper to the other side of that fence, no matter the fence or the barrier we put in place, if Cooper wanted to get out, he would do everything he could to get out.

Though we have the Holy Spirit of God, we, as Christians, still wrestle with a corrupt nature. We carefully position fences, barriers, and stakes (or whatever metaphor you want to use for "boundaries"). However, if we put those boundaries in place and think those things alone will do the trick, we will be sadly mistaken and incredibly discouraged. Fences can still be dug under, hopped, or climbed out of if you want what is on the other side bad enough.

You may struggle with the temptation of anger and are doing everything you can to be less angry using your own strength. You're listening to peaceful music, practicing breathing techniques, exercising more, and working fewer hours, yet you still find yourself coming home and lashing out at your kids or spouse. You selfishly think, *"They don't understand what I do for them,"* and then you give in to your anger, throw stuff, yell at them, and make your family and the people around you feel unsafe.

Maybe your temptation is with drunkenness. It constantly calls for you, and you say "no" to a drink one day, and the next day, the temptation returns. You avoid driving by the liquor store and going to bars with your friends now. Maybe you've gone to rehab and thought that would fix it. And next thing you know, you've consumed six drinks within an hour, and you're completely out of control. Right back where you began.

Maybe you're tempted by greed. You try to budget, put holds on your account, say that you'll tithe more, and try not to scam any of your clients to make a few extra dollars. And repeatedly, you walk by that purse, car, or pair of shoes you want, and you think, *"Oh, I so deserve this."*

Maybe you are struggling with sexual temptation. Perhaps you have been in a battle with pornography for years. No matter how many passcodes you put on your phone, how many websites you block on your computer, or how many numbers you delete, you still fall into the lie of *"No one's going to know."* You find yourself giving into these desires, and you're living in the hidden shame of it. Maybe you're having an affair with someone on a screen or in real life, and you don't know what else to do. You've put all the fences up that you could think of, but, like Cooper, you keep getting out of the backyard.

Christian, the Bible teaches that we naturally want what is on the other side of the fence more than we want God. We face temptations because we want what we cannot have, and our hearts naturally want to pursue those temptations more than we want to pursue our Heavenly Father. The ultimate way to achieve true and lasting resistance is not a change of boundaries or a change of reason. It is a change of your heart.

This passage does not teach, *"Look at Joseph's ability to reason, his discipline, self-control, and resolve."* And it doesn't teach those things because, on his own, Joseph is like you and me. We cannot naturally love God on our own and honor Him.

So, what do we do?

Above all, we must grow in our love for God and bring our hearts closer to Him.

Joseph did not resist Potiphar's wife because he was naturally a great guy. While he did put up wise fences and boundaries, his hope and perseverance were not rooted in them. Joseph's foundation for resisting temptation was a deep love for God and His ways, to the point where he says to Potiphar's wife, "How could I do this great wickedness and sin against God?"

Notice how he didn't say "no" out of a "religious obligation." He didn't say, "I'm a follower of Yahweh, and this just goes against my beliefs." He didn't say to her, "Thank you for your offer, but I really shouldn't." This would be like the high school student hanging out with the wrong crowd and their friends asking them to do something they probably shouldn't. Their reasons might be:

1. "I want to, but my parents said I shouldn't stay out late."

2. "I'm not allowed to; my parents said I shouldn't."

By the way, if you happen to be in high school, these are good reasons to say "no!" Trust your parents. But let's consider these reasons and their lack of conviction. How fragile can that be? How much can our reason be swayed if we are only trying to follow a set of rules or obligations without any kind of love and devotion?

Joseph's unwavering resistance to temptation was not the result of fear or obligation but a testament to his deep love and trust in God. In the same way, high schoolers should learn to say "no" to negative influences out of love and trust in their parents. "I love my Father; how could I possibly go against Him?" This should be the guiding principle in our lives, leading us to resist temptation and make choices that align with our faith.

UNDERSTANDING OUR SIN

If we are going to resist temptations in our lives and live for God's glory, we must love God above everything else. And we must grow in this love, drawing nearer to Him in prayer and letting Him speak to us through His Word. As we grow in our love for God, we also see our sin more for what it is. This does not mean that we count up all the bad things we have done in our lives, write them down on paper, and then sulk over those things that we have done. It doesn't mean we forever live in a place of guilt and shame and always feel bad about ourselves.

As we grow in love for God, we come to a profound realization of our nature and our sinful hearts. We acknowledge that, on our own, we have sinned and fallen short of God's glory. This understanding is not a result of our efforts alone but a testament to the Biblical truth that we are incapable of loving God for who He is without His divine assistance. This is the essence of our spiritual journey: to understand our need for God's love and guidance.

> And **you were dead in the trespasses** and sins in which you once walked, following the course of this world, following the prince of the power of the air, the spirit that is now at work in the sons of disobedience—among whom we all once lived in the passions of our flesh, carrying out the desires of the body and the mind, and were by nature children of wrath, like the rest of mankind.
> (Ephesians 2:1-3)

The truth is we are dead in our trespasses. And if we do not understand how wretched and undeserving we really are, we will not fully appreciate how truly great God's love is for us!

THE GIFT OF HIS SON, JESUS

Once we face our sins, we can truly appreciate the magnitude of God's love for us. It is a love that is not earned but freely given, as evidenced in the gift of His Son.

> In this is love, not that we have loved God but that he loved us and sent his Son to be the propitiation for our sins.
> (1 John 4:10)

When we can see our sin and comprehend the hopelessness of our human condition, we can look at Jesus Christ and see that, though we were undeserving of forgiveness and did not deserve God's love, He still loved us and gave us His Son. When we understand that it was supposed to be us on the cross instead of Jesus Christ, we begin to understand how deep God's love for us truly goes.

While Joseph did not see Christ in his earthly life, he certainly saw God's presence and God's love in his life. He saw God's love for him through the mercy and the blessings he was given, and because he saw God's love for him, he responded in love.

OUR RESPONSE TO GOD'S LOVE

We respond to God's love for us in love. Joseph saw God's love, and when Potiphar's wife tempted him to sin against God, he responded, "How could I ever go against God, my Father?" He responded to God's love with love. We are called to do the same.

"We love because he [God] first loved us."
(1 John 4:19)

Loving God is not dependent on our natural ability to love because, if so, we would be hopeless. Loving God is looking at Jesus on the cross, seeing His love for you, and letting His love for you drive your love for Him. Any love you have for God is simply a response to God's gracious and incredible love for you. Ultimately, Joseph's natural love for God did not lead him to flee from sin. It was God's love for Joseph that kept Joseph obedient and untouched by sin. Joseph simply responded to God's love for him, and this loving God protected Joseph from himself.

PRAYERFULLY ASK FOR WISDOM

Joseph had strategies and boundaries, but the only reason he was faithful within those boundaries was because of God's love for him and his response to God's love. So, as we grow in God's love and begin to understand how deep His love is for us, let us continue to grow in love for Him. Let us repeatedly ask God to provide the wisdom and the strategies to succeed at resisting our temptations.

In response to God's love for you, perhaps phones and laptops must be given up! Maybe liquor bottles need to be thrown in the trash! Possibly, biblical counseling is something that needs to be pursued. Many terrific biblical counseling ministries are available to those seeking a healthy change. Young people, perhaps an honest conversation with your parent or parents needs to happen! Maybe it's time to reach out for help to confront your sinful struggles and desires as you continue to strive to love God more.

Parents, there are many ways to create support for your teenager's walk with God. The journey must begin; the first step (reaching out) must be taken. God has called you to be the primary disciplers, and we, as the church, want to equip you further to disciple your kids in a manner that honors God. We want to partner with you to help your young people grow in their love for God, which will help them learn to resist temptations through loving Christ. Let us recognize God's love for us, respond to His love in love for Him, and prayerfully fight our temptations, not just with our own will and strategies, but with His love.

CONCLUSION

Perhaps some are reading this who are on the brink of giving in to a temptation that, if they stop resisting, can be devastating to themselves, their careers, their marriages, their kids, and most importantly, their souls.

I urge you in this moment to consider the love of God. Consider Jesus, the Son of God, who died for your sins so that you may have freedom and eternal life in Him—free from sin. In Him, you will be truly satisfied. In Him is where your life truly belongs.

Even though Joseph resisted sin, he still lost everything on this earth. Potiphar's wife falsely accused him of trying to sleep with her. Potiphar believed her, and Joseph ended up getting thrown into prison and lost everything he had, but he still had God.

> **But the Lord was with Joseph** and
> *showed him steadfast love and gave him*
> *favor in the sight of the keeper of the prison.*
> (Genesis 39:21)

Joseph still had God, who showed him steadfast love in prison. You may lose something dear to your sinful heart if you walk away from your temptations, but I urge you to walk away so that you may still have God.

You may believe that the grass is not greener on the other side of resisting temptation. You may think that living in this sin is like a green pasture. But I pray that by the grace of God, you understand you are living in a desert, hallucinating, dying, and you need the Living Water. The only way for you to leave this wasteland of sin is by putting your faith in Jesus Christ for the forgiveness of your sins and the deliverance from your old and sinful heart. And as you see God's love for you on display at the cross and realize that

God is better than the desert you were living in, you are able to respond in love for Him and delight in His ways more than your own.

I invite you to come to Jesus, experience God's love for you, and, as a response, turn away from your sins.

Now to him who is able to keep you from stumbling and to present you blameless before the presence of his glory with great joy, to the only God, our Savior, through Jesus Christ our Lord, be glory, majesty, dominion, and authority, before all time and now and forever. Amen.
(Jude 24-25)

PRAYER

Father, we thank you for your deep, deep love for us. It is not that we loved you first but that you loved us and gave your Son Jesus on our behalf. We pray that everyone reading these words grows in their love for you and that we all see you as the perfect, loving Heavenly Father you are. As we see your love, Father, help us to respond to that love with love and devotion to You. For any of us struggling with temptations, we pray that we no longer rely solely on our own strategies or abilities and that we come to grips with the fact that we can't resist temptation alone. We can't walk with you and honor you on our own. But Lord, you offer to hold your children fast. Instead of relying on ourselves, help us, Lord, to consider Your love for us so that we may draw nearer to You and walk in the ways of Your gracious calling. We love you, Lord, and pray all this in Jesus' name. Amen.

ABOUT CLIMBING ANGEL PUBLISHING

Climbing Angel Publishing shares stories of hope and encouragement, aids in the gathering together of community, and supports the process of betterment. The following books are available at your leading online bookstores.

ADULT BOOKS: (Romans 8:28-30)

In His Image by Sam Polson
(English, Romanian, & Mandarin)
By Faith by Sam Polson (English & Romanian)
My Birthday Gift to Jesus by Lisa Soland
Without Ceasing by Dr. Dennis Davidson
SonLight: Daily Light from the Pages of God's Word
by Sam Polson
Corona Victus: Conquering the Virus of Fear
by Sam Polson (English & Romanian)
*Art Bushing: His Diary, Letters, & Photographs of
WWII* by Art Bushing
*Art & Dotty: His Diary, Their Letters & Photographs of
WWII* by Art Bushing
Trimisul by Stan Johnson (Romanian)
Life Changing Prayer by Sam Polson
The Climbing Angel Christmas Treasury,
variety of authors
J. Calvin Coolidge: Letters from the Korean War
by J. Calvin Coolidge
*Stories from Kingman, AZ: The Heart of Historic Route
66* by Loren B. Wilson
*Pathways: Ancient Paths from the Pages of the Old
Testament* by Sam Polson

THE SINGLE SERMON SERIES:
(1 Peter 3:15)

Jesus is Alive! by Mike Sager
My Mother's Bible by Sam Polson
The Lost Boys by Jake Bishop
Melchizedek: A Shadow of Christ by Jerry Scheumann
A Servant of Christ by James Alan Lynch
Dreaming God's Dream by Dr. Al Cage
Resisting Sin by Colin Hughes

CHILDREN'S BOOKS: (Philippians 4:8)

The Christmas Tree Angel by Lisa Soland
The Unmade Moose by Lisa Soland
Thump by Lisa Soland
Somebunny To Love by Lisa Soland
(English & Mandarin)
The Truth About God's Rainbow by Lisa Soland
God's Promises by Lisa Soland
The Boy & The Bagel Necklace by Lisa Soland
God's Hands and Feet by Lisa Soland
I Like To Be Quiet by Joni Caldwell
Wheels Off! by Karlie Saumier
Ella's Trip of a Lifetime by Melanie Ewbank
Because You Are Mine by Gayle Childress Greene
Jeremy Plays the Blues by Amy Oden Simpson
Bad Hair Day by Jasmyne Simpkins
I Like To Read by Joni Caldwell
Trunks Up! by Karlie Saumier
Perusha's Paradise by Bette Reed Smith
Ruby and the Treasure Within
by Tonya Celeste Hobbs
Abby, the Wonder Dog & her Warrior Princess
by Melanie Ewbank
The Christmas Coat by Lisa Soland
Danger Around the Bend by Karlie Saumier

www.ingramcontent.com/pod-product-compliance
Lightning Source LLC
Chambersburg PA
CBHW051604120626
46551CB00013B/1662

* 9 7 8 1 9 5 6 2 1 8 3 8 1 *